Easy, Fabulous Bread Making
A collection of quick, no-knead, homemade bread recipes

by

Barbara Mack

Yes, I wrote this book for you. But you already knew that.

A beautiful loaf of bread, fresh from the oven.

The Search for Good Bread

Bread.

It's one of the most important foods in the diet of man. Riots have started over its lack, it has been the catalyst for revolutions, and even today there is violence on the streets in some countries when the price of bread goes up too quickly. Before the French Revolution, when the peasants were rioting in the streets because they had no bread to eat, Marie Antoinette is supposed to have said: 'Then let them eat cake'. If she did say this (and there is some doubt as to whether she actually did or not), she was almost certainly referring to brioche, a rich bread that contains eggs and butter.

Close your eyes and imagine the smell of fresh bread wafting under your nose. Are you smiling yet? One of life's greatest pleasures is sinking your teeth into a buttery slice of crusty bread, still warm from the oven.

And yet there is, especially in the United States, almost a universal carelessness about the quality and taste of the bread that we eat on a daily basis. People eat the most appalling trash imaginable, and accept it as a matter of course. The normal bread in an American household is a pasty white bread that is more air than food, devoid of nutrients, and stuffed with chemicals so it has a longer shelf life.

And it tastes bad.

I don't like things that taste bad.

So instead of disgusting white bread, I tried eating whole wheat bread from the store, and some of it was better. I could still taste the chemicals in it, though. Then I tried only eating bakery bread. It was better still. Tasted great, but it was expensive. I couldn't afford to pay four or five dollars for every loaf of bread I bought. I tried making my own bread, and it was good - sometimes. It was always a toss-up whether the bread was going to rise enough, or if I'd kneaded it long enough, and really, I didn't have time to make a loaf of bread every time we needed some. I worked, I had kids, and like most everyone else, I struggled to find the time to do the things I already did.

So I bought a bread maker, and waited impatiently for the first loaf to come out. I was disappointed, however; the bread was too heavy and dense, and it had a harsh yeast taste. Why didn't the bread I bought from bakeries taste that way? Wasn't it made in the same manner? With some experimentation, I found that if I made the dough in the bread maker but did the second rise *outside* the bread maker and then baked it in the oven, the bread was better. The texture became lighter, but it still tasted too harsh.

Then Jim Lahey of the Sullivan Street Bakery in New York came out with a recipe that used minimal yeast and required no kneading. The bread had a better flavor because of the long, slow rise on the counter top, but I didn't like the texture. Something was off. Sadly, I wrote that recipe off and went back to making bread only on special occasions.

Then one day while I was making bread, I got called away just as I stirred all the ingredients together. I covered the bowl and threw it in the refrigerator. I found the forgotten dough the next day, and was intrigued to see that it had still risen, even in the cold. I didn't think it would be any good, but I hate to throw anything away. So I punched the dough down, shaped it into a rough loaf, let it do a second rise, and put it in the oven.

It was the best bread I'd ever made.

It had a complex flavor, no harsh yeast taste, and the loaf was crusty on the outside and light on the inside. I shared it with company, and they raved over it. So I tried it again, this time reducing the amount of yeast that I'd used, but not as much as it had been reduced in Jim Lahey's recipe. And yet again, I made a great-tasting loaf of bread, without any kneading and without any bother.

Usually, when you make bread, you have to knead it and let it rise, then punch it down and let it rise again. You have to hope you've kneaded it for long enough to develop the gluten, and the whole process takes a long time. If you don't let it rise long enough, the texture (or crumb) of the bread is heavy, it doesn't hold together very well, and it's not as tasty. When you let it rise too long, the bread will fall in the heat of the oven, again making it heavy...and not as tasty.

Here's why kneading is usually necessary: During the normal kneading process, the gluten in your dough begins to form and strengthen. Gluten is what holds the loaf of bread together so that it doesn't fall apart during baking. The flour absorbs the water, and as you knead, it becomes stretchy. The gluten creates small air pockets in the dough, and bubbles of carbon dioxide form in the air pockets. That's what causes the stretchy dough to rise and gives your bread a light, airy texture.

When I put the bread dough in the refrigerator and forgot about it for about 24 hours, the gluten developed just as it does during kneading, and the dough still became stretchy. But here's something else that happened during the slow rise in the cold of the refrigerator – the flavors of the bread developed and intensified. I tested this new way of making bread, again and again. It came out perfectly, every single time. After some more experimenting, I even came up with a way to skip the second rise completely. That's right. You can put the bread dough straight from the refrigerator into the oven, and it gives you a perfectly risen, great-tasting loaf of bread, every time. You can stir together the dough right before bedtime, then when you get home from work the next day, you can take it out and bake a loaf of bread to serve with dinner.

This bread is so easy and so cheap to make, I haven't eaten store-bought bread in more than two years. I've become spoiled, and I will never eat bad bread again. After trying some of these recipes, you may very well say the same thing.

Tips, Tricks, and Important Things to Know

Bread flour is the best flour you can use in these recipes. It tastes better, and it rises better. But if this isn't available, or if it costs too much for you, plain old unbleached all-purpose flour will be just fine.

These recipes are going to produce a dough that is a little wetter and stickier than what you ordinarily see.

You're going to use approximately one-half to three-quarters the amount of yeast that you normally use in a bread recipe. Rapid rise or bread machine yeast is best. If you use regular yeast, you need to proof it by adding it to the warm water of the recipe along with a little sugar (whatever amount is in the recipe, or if there is no sugar in the recipe, add a tsp of it to the warm water) and leaving it for ten minutes until it becomes foamy. If it doesn't foam, you're going to have to throw it out and use different yeast. Using rapid rise or bread machine yeast lets you skip this step.

Once the ingredients in the recipe are stirred together, cover the bowl with plastic wrap or a lid and put it in the refrigerator. **Make sure that the lid is not airtight.** The dough needs to stay in the refrigerator and rise for at least 8 hours, up to five days. You can pinch off and bake on an as-needed basis.

If you want to freeze the dough, let it rise for 8 hours first in the refrigerator. Then deflate the dough and make it into a ball, wrap it in plastic, **and put it in an airtight container** in the freezer. You can keep it frozen for up to three months. When you want to use it, just take it from the freezer and let it thaw. Then let it rise until doubled in size, and bake it for the same amount of time stated in the recipe, at the same temperature recommended in the recipe.

If you think your bread is taking too long to rise or it hasn't risen high enough, don't worry. Put the pan on the stove while it preheats and that will help the rise. Let it rise until the dough doesn't spring back when you press it. It may take a while, because the dough has to come to room temperature first. Don't worry if it doesn't appear to be completely doubled in size: **You can always force a higher rise by turning the oven twenty-five degrees higher for the first ten minutes of the baking time.**

*****Time saving technique***** If you don't have time to let the loaf of bread rise a second time, shape the dough into a boule (round loaf) and put it into a greased, heavy pan with a lid. You don't even have to let the oven preheat. Just turn the oven 40 degrees above the temp recommended in the recipe. Bake the bread for the amount of time stated in the recipe; then turn the oven down to the original temp, take the lid off the pan, and let the bread cook for ten more minutes, or until it browns. This will make crusty bread, as it steams the bread during cooking.

If your bread crust gets too chewy, put it in a plastic bag after it cools completely and the crust will soften. Likewise, if you want to keep it chewy, store the bread in a paper bag.

Always wait at least 20 minutes for the bread to cool before cutting it. Otherwise, the steam trapped inside the bread will make the bread doughy.

If you want a chewy crust on your bread, either put a shallow pan of water on the second shelf of your oven while your bread bakes, or spray-mist water onto the sides and door of the oven two or three times in the first five minutes of cooking time.

Farmhouse white bread, cooled and sliced. Look at the chewy crust, and the soft interior. Mmm.

Farmhouse White Bread

1 cup warm water
½ cup milk
½ cup melted butter, cooled
3 T sugar
1 tsp salt
2 tsp yeast*
4 cups flour

Stir all dry ingredients together in large bowl. Add all wet ingredients. Stir with wooden spoon until well-mixed (about five minutes) but do not knead. Cover bowl lightly with plastic wrap or lid and place in refrigerator overnight or for at least 8 hours. Dough can remain in refrigerator for up to 5 days.

Take cold dough out of refrigerator. You may need to oil or flour your hands, as the dough can stick to you. Divide dough in half, and stretch out to fit roughly in a well-oiled loaf pan. Alternatively, you may form into round boules (by stretching the ends underneath) and place on a baking sheet scattered with corn meal to keep loaves from sticking. Cover, and let rise in a warm place until doubled. Dough is ready when you can touch it and the indention remains. If it doesn't spring back, it's ready. You may want to brush the top with butter to promote browning and give it a delicious taste.*

Bake at 350F for about 30 minutes. When done, bread will sound hollow when thumped. Let cool at least 20 minutes before slicing.

*If not using rapid rise or bread machine yeast, add sugar to warm water and sprinkle with yeast. Wait ten minutes for it to foam, then proceed with recipe. If it doesn't foam, throw it out and start over.

*If you want a chewy crust on your bread, either put a shallow pan of water on the second shelf of your oven while your bread bakes, or spray-mist water onto the sides and door of the oven two or three times in the first five minutes of cooking time.

A soft, delicious potato roll, just waiting for you to pull it apart and slather with butter.

Potato Rolls

These are a huge hit around my house. I make them every time I make mashed potatoes, and sometimes I boil up a little potato and mash it with a fork in the water just so that I can make rolls. Potato water, by the way, is just water that you've boiled potatoes in. If you don't have enough, just add water to the amount that you have. You can also just add a heaping tablespoon of instant potatoes to the water instead.

1 ¼ cups (cooled to lukewarm) potato water (or 1 1/4 cup water with 1 T instant potatoes added)
¼ cup sugar
1 tsp salt
2 tsp yeast*
2 beaten eggs
½ cup softened butter
4 cups flour

Mix everything except flour in large bowl. Beat in half of the flour. Stir well, then beat in remaining flour and stir for about 5 minutes. This is a very sticky, tacky dough. Cover and refrigerate at least 8 hours or up to 5 days.

When you want to bake them, pinch off a small portion, shape into a ball and place (barely touching) in a greased pan or on an oiled cooking sheet. You might have to oil or flour your hands to roll them into balls. Cover with a kitchen towel, and let rise until doubled. Before baking, brush with butter or milk to promote browning. Don't use an egg white wash; this is a soft roll, and egg washes tend to make rolls harder on top. You don't want a chewy crust on these.

Bake at 350F for about 20 minutes. No two people make their rolls the same size, so check for doneness after 15 minutes. You might even have to eat a roll, or two, to check.

*If not using rapid rise or bread machine yeast, add sugar to warm water and sprinkle with yeast. Wait ten minutes for it to foam, then proceed with recipe. If it doesn't foam, throw it out and start over.

Hawaiian bread, cooling while I wait impatiently.

Hawaiian Bread

1 cup pineapple juice
1 cup water
½ cup sugar
1 ½ tsp salt
2 tsp yeast*
½ tsp ground ginger
1 tsp vanilla
½ cup butter
2 eggs
5 cups flour

Mix half of the flour with the rest of the ingredients. Beat it well, until thoroughly mixed. Add in remaining flour and mix well again, but do not knead. Cover loosely and refrigerate for at least 8 hours or up to 5 days.

When ready to bake, divide dough in half and form into round boules by turning the ends underneath and placing seam-side down in an oiled ovenproof pan. Let rise until doubled; slash an X in the top of the loaf. Bake at 350 F for 25-30 minutes.

*If not using rapid rise or bread machine yeast, add sugar to warm water and sprinkle with yeast. Wait ten minutes for it to foam, then proceed with recipe. If it doesn't foam, throw it out and start over.

A lovely baton of French bread.

French Bread

1 tsp yeast*
1 cup water
2 T sugar
1 ½ tsp salt
3 T vegetable oil
3 cups flour

Mix all ingredients together and stir well. Cover and refrigerate for at least 8 hours, up to 5 days.

Divide dough in half for two large loaves, or in four pieces for small ones. Roll out into a rectangle on floured surface until approximately ½ inch thick. Roll tightly from large end to large end and pinch to seal. Seal ends the same way. Place seam side down on oiled baking sheet (or sprinkle cornmeal on it, instead) and let rise until doubled. Make diagonal slashes before putting in oven (it releases steam while baking). If you want the bread nice and browned, brush the loaves with an egg white beaten with a T of water before baking. Bake at 400F for 5 minutes, then turn oven down to 350F and bake for 20 more. (Cooking times are for two large batons, and may have to be adjusted slightly if you make four small ones.) Let cool for at least twenty minutes.

*If not using rapid rise or bread machine yeast, add sugar to warm water and sprinkle with yeast. Wait ten minutes for it to foam, then proceed with recipe. If it doesn't foam, throw it out and start over.

The molasses in the recipe give this Anadama bread a lovely flavor and color.

New England Anadama Bread
(can be made with or without blueberries)

1 ¼ cup boiling water
¼ cup cornmeal
¼ cup molasses
3 T butter
1 tsp yeast*
1 tsp salt
1 cup frozen blueberries *Optional*
3 cups flour

Stir together boiling water, cornmeal, molasses, salt, and butter. Whisk until there are no lumps, and leave to cool until barely warm. Stir in blueberries (if using), yeast, and flour, and mix thoroughly. Cover and refrigerate for at least 8 hours and up to 5 days.

Divide dough into two and shape into boules by turning the ends under and placing seam down on oiled or cornmeal scattered cooking sheet. Cover and let rise until doubled. Bake at 375F for about 30 minutes. Let cool at least twenty minutes.

*If not using rapid rise or bread machine yeast, add sugar to warm water and sprinkle with yeast. Wait ten minutes for it to foam, then proceed with recipe. If it doesn't foam, throw it out and start over.

*If using berries and have fresh, just place them in the freezer for an hour prior to making bread. Freezing them keeps them from bursting while you stir together the ingredients.

Onion and garlic bagels. Yum.

Bagels

1 tsp yeast*
1 T brown sugar
1 T vegetable oil
1 tsp salt
¾ cup water
2 ½ cups flour
½ to 1 cup optional ingredients

Mix all ingredients together and beat thoroughly. This makes a little stiffer dough, so you may have to work it in with your hands, but do not knead. This recipe is extremely versatile, and you can add ½ to 1 cup of anything to it at this point, to make the kinds of bagels you like best. The bagels shown in the picture have about a ½ cup of browned chopped onion and some garlic added.

Cover and put in refrigerator for at least 8 hours, for up to 5 days.

Divide into twelve pieces and make into balls. Roll with your hands into an approximately 6 inch long snake and bring ends together to form a circle, pinching to seal the ends.

Meanwhile, bring a large pot of salted water to a rolling boil. Drop the dough circles in one or two at a time, flipping them over to make sure that they cook about a minute on each side. Transfer to a towel, and then place on an oiled cooking sheet. If you want to add a topping (poppy seeds, cinnamon and sugar, etc) do it now, while the bagel is still wet. Bake at 350F for 20 minutes or until golden brown. This makes 12 medium to small size bagels, or 8 large.

*If not using rapid rise or bread machine yeast, add sugar to warm water and sprinkle with yeast. Wait ten minutes for it to foam, then proceed with recipe. If it doesn't foam, throw it out and start over.

Blueberry Coffee Cake

Coffee Cake

Coffee Cake:
1 ¼ cups water
1 tsp yeast*
1 tsp salt
¼ cup vegetable oil
¼ cup sugar
2 ¾ cups flour

Streusel topping:
½ cup brown sugar
¾ cup flour
1 T cinnamon
½ cup melted butter
1 tsp vanilla

~ Optional fruit topping
20 oz can of pie filling *or*
2 cups fresh or frozen fruit or berries
cooked until thick with
½ cup sugar &
¼ cup water

~ Optional cheese topping
1 package cream cheese, softened (8 oz)
1 beaten egg
¼ cup sugar

Add all coffee cake ingredients together and mix thoroughly. Mix streusel topping ingredients in separate, small bowl. Cover both and refrigerate at least 8 hours or up to 5 days.

Spread and stretch dough into greased 9 X 13 pan. Use a fork to thoroughly fluff and separate streusel topping. If not using other, optional toppings, spread streusel evenly and thickly over top of dough.

~ If using fruit topping: Spread half of streusel topping over dough, then pour pie filling or (cooled) cooked fruit mixture over top. Sprinkle with remaining streusel.

~ If using cheese topping: Mix softened cream cheese with egg and sugar. Sprinkle half of streusel topping over dough, then spread cheese topping over it. Sprinkle with remaining streusel.

Cover and let rise in warm place until doubled. Bake at 350F for about 35 to 40 minutes. Let cool at least twenty minutes before serving.

*If not using rapid rise or bread machine yeast, add sugar to warm water and sprinkle with yeast. Wait ten minutes for it to foam, then proceed with recipe. If it doesn't foam, throw it out and start over.

Pinto bean bread: the best sandwich bread, ever.

Pinto Bean Bread

This is a great way to use up leftover beans. I like this bread so well, I often put aside cooked beans to ensure that I'll be able to make it. Please don't let food prejudices stop you from trying it.

½ cup cooked and mashed pinto beans
1 cup water
¼ cup milk
1 ½ tsp salt
1 T sugar
2 tsp yeast
2 T vegetable or olive oil
3 cups flour

Mix all ingredients except flour together in large bowl. Add in half the flour; beat well. Add in remaining flour and mix thoroughly, but do not knead. Cover and refrigerate for at least 8 hours, for up to 5 days.

Shape into one large or two small loaves or boules. Cover and let rise until doubled. Bake at 350F for 45 minutes (for one large loaf) or 30 minutes for two smaller loaves. When you thump the bottom of the loaf, it should sound hollow.

Rustic gourmet crackers, topped with sea salt and cracked black pepper.

Gourmet Whole Grain Crackers

½ cup whole wheat flour
¼ cup unbleached, all-purpose flour
½ tsp salt
¼ tsp yeast
1 T oil
1 T honey
¼ cup warm water plus 2 T

Mix all dry ingredients together in medium bowl. Mix honey, oil, and water in a cup and then stir into dry ingredients. Mix thoroughly, then cover and refrigerate for at least two hours, or up to 5 days.

Drop dough onto floured surface, and cover with towel. Let come to room temperature, then separate into three balls. Flatten balls, and roll them out into very thin rectangles. You want this dough so thin, you could almost see through it.

Transfer dough to oiled baking sheets, and spritz with water. You can then sprinkle with any toppings you like: sea salt, poppy seeds, cracked black or red pepper, or even grated Parmesan cheese. Bake at 350F for about 20 minutes, or until crackers are lightly browned. Let cool completely, then break into rough crackers.

Honey flax seed bread.

Honey Flax Seed Bread

1 ½ cups water
½ cup honey
1 ½ tsp salt
2 tsp yeast*
¼ cup softened butter
4 heaping T ground flax seed
4 cups flour

Mix half the flour together with all other ingredients. Beat thoroughly, until well mixed. Beat in other half of flour. Cover, then refrigerate for at least 8 hours or up to 5 days.

Makes two smaller loaves, or one large one. If making two, divide dough into two pieces. Stretch to roughly fit an oiled loaf pan, or form into a round boule and put on a baking sheet. Cover and let rise until doubled. Bake at 350F for 40-45 minutes for one large loaf, 30 minutes for two small. Let cool at least twenty minutes.

*If not using rapid rise or bread machine yeast, add sugar to warm water and sprinkle with yeast. Wait ten minutes for it to foam, then proceed with recipe. If it doesn't foam, throw it out and start over.

English Muffins

This is a recipe that seems hard, but really isn't. You don't bake English muffins, you steam them. It's a dough that's wet enough to scoop, and you cook it in a ring. (In this case, it's the ring from a canning jar, which is what I had lying around.) I've seen other recipes where the muffins were cut out with a biscuit cutter, but I've tried several of those, and none of them were good. Too dry. In the case of English muffins, the wetter the dough, the better.

1 cup water
1/3 cup milk
1 T sugar
1 T softened butter
1 tsp salt
2 tsp yeast
2 cups flour

Other things needed:
skillet with a lid
metal rings, such as those used on canning jars

Mix all the ingredients together and beat thoroughly with a wooden spoon, for at least 5 minutes. Cover and refrigerate for at least 2 hours, for up to 5 days.

Heat a skillet with a lid over medium heat. Place the metal rings in the skillet and coat lightly with vegetable spray. Fill each ring about ¾ full and cover the pan with a lid. Cook for about 5 minutes. Remove the lid and flip the rings. Using tongs is the easiest way, but you can do it with a spatula. Cover again with lid, and cook 5 more minutes, or until they're golden brown. Place on a cooling rack, remove the rings and let cool for about ten minutes. Split with a fork and serve.

*This recipe doesn't really require a lot of rising time in the refrigerator or out of it. I usually make the dough the night before, and then cook the muffins in the morning. If you want to make the muffins right then, just let the dough rise in a warm place, covered, for about half an hour. Then proceed with the rest of the recipe.

See all the nooks and crannies in these lovely muffins?

Surprisingly easy to make, these English muffins make a wonderful breakfast, especially topped with fresh fruit.

Healthy Cinnamon Raisin Bread

Unlike most sweet breads, this version of the ever-popular Cinnamon Raisin Bread is actually good for you. Full of healthy grains like oatmeal and flax seed, it makes a wonderfully filling breakfast. Because cinnamon reduces rise, this recipe contains a little extra yeast.

1 ½ cups water
½ cup honey or sugar
1 cup raisins, soaked in 1 cup water
¼ cup butter
1 ½ cup oats, either quick or old fashioned
4 T ground flax seed
1 tsp salt
3 tsp yeast*
1 T cinnamon
4 ½ cups flour

Put raisins in a small bowl, and cover with 1 cup water. Let them soak for at least a half hour. Meanwhile, combine all other ingredients and half the flour in a large bowl. Beat for about 5 minutes with a wooden spoon. When raisins have finished soaking, add them and their liquid, along with the rest of the flour, to the bowl. Mix thoroughly. Cover and refrigerate for at least 8 hours, for up to 5 days.

Divide dough, and form into two loaves or round boules and place on oiled baking sheet or in greased loaf pan. Cover, and let rise until doubled. Bake at 350F for 45 minutes. Let cool completely before slicing.

*If not using rapid rise or bread machine yeast, add sugar to warm water and sprinkle with yeast. Wait ten minutes for it to foam, then proceed with recipe. If it doesn't foam, throw it out and start over.

Portuguese Sweet Bread

1 cup milk
1 egg
2 T softened butter
1/3 cup sugar
1 tsp salt
3 cups flour
1 tsp yeast*

Mix all ingredients together in large bowl; beat well with wooden spoon. Cover bowl and place in refrigerator for at least 8 hours, for up to 5 days.

Shape into round boule by stretching ends underneath and place seam side down on oiled baking sheet. Cover, and let rise until doubled. Bake at 375F for 30-35 minutes.

*If not using rapid rise or bread machine yeast, add sugar to warm water and sprinkle with yeast. Wait ten minutes for it to foam, then proceed with recipe. If it doesn't foam, throw it out and start over.

Chewy, delicious crust. You'll never buy pizza again with this easy recipe.

Pizza Crust

Once you get a load of this easy, delicious pizza dough, you will never buy pizza again. Like me, you'll become addicted to this easy recipe. It can be easily frozen, either still in a ball or already rolled out into a pizza shape. Just make sure that you let it rise in the refrigerator first, then put it in an airtight container to freeze it.

1 cup water
1 T sugar
1 tsp yeast*
3 T olive oil
1 tsp salt
2 ½ cups flour

Mix all ingredients together thoroughly in large bowl. Cover, and refrigerate for 8 hours or up to 5 days.

Let come to room temperature, then either roll out to desired size crust, or alternatively, pat dough into an oiled cooking sheet or on a pizza stone. If desired, sprinkle basil, thyme, or garlic onto crust. Garnish with your favorite pizza toppings and bake for 15 to 20 minutes in a preheated 425F oven.

*If not using rapid rise or bread machine yeast, add sugar to warm water and sprinkle with yeast. Wait ten minutes for it to foam, then proceed with recipe. If it doesn't foam, throw it out and start over.

Wonderful White Bread

This is a basic bread recipe for white bread, but when you take it out of the oven, you won't ever think of white bread as 'plain' anymore. This recipe makes a very soft, tasty loaf with a chewy crust. Great for sandwiches, it's incredibly easy to make and requires just a few ingredients.

1 cup water
2 T sugar
1 ½ tsp yeast*
1 tsp salt
¼ cup vegetable oil
3 cups flour

Mix all ingredients thoroughly in large bowl. Cover, and refrigerate for 8 hours or up to 5 days.

Stretch dough to roughly fit an oiled loaf pan. Cover and let rise until doubled, then bake at 375F for 30-35 minutes. Let cool at least twenty minutes before slicing.

*If not using rapid rise or bread machine yeast, add sugar to warm water and sprinkle with yeast. Wait ten minutes for it to foam, then proceed with recipe. If it doesn't foam, throw it out and start over.

Focaccia Bread

1 cup water
¼ cup olive oil
1 tsp salt
1 clove minced garlic
2 tsp dried rosemary
2 tsp sugar
1 tsp yeast*
3 cups flour

*topping for focaccia bread
olive oil
rosemary (optional)
grated Parmesan cheese (optional)
Kosher or sea salt
basil (optional)
any other herb you might like (optional)

Thoroughly mix all ingredients in large bowl. Cover, and refrigerate for at least 8 hours, for up to 5 days.

Let come to room temperature, then pat dough into either a 9 X 13 inch baking pan or 12 inch pizza pan. Use your fingers to dimple the dough every inch or so. Drizzle olive oil over bread, letting it pool in dimples occasionally. Sprinkle with Kosher or sea salt, and any herb or cheese you desire. Bake at 400F for 20-25 minutes. Let cool at least 5 minutes before serving.

*If not using rapid rise or bread machine yeast, add sugar to warm water and sprinkle with yeast. Wait ten minutes for it to foam, then proceed with recipe. If it doesn't foam, throw it out and start over.

Cardamom Bread

This bread is often made at special occasions, but it can be enjoyed any time of the year. The wonderful aroma will waft through the house while it's baking, making you crazy to sample it. And if it lasts long enough to get a little stale, it makes great French toast.

1 egg
½ cup milk
½ cup applesauce
¼ cup honey
1 tsp salt
1 ½ tsp yeast*
1 tsp cardamom
2 ½ cups flour

Mix all ingredients thoroughly in large bowl. Cover, and refrigerate for at least 8 hours, and up to 5 days.

Shape into a loaf or boule, and place in oiled loaf pan or on greased baking sheet. Cover, and let rise until doubled. Brush top of loaf with water and bake at 350F for 40 minutes. Loaf will sound hollow when the bottom is tapped. Let cool in pan for about 15 minutes, then move to rack and let cool another hour before slicing.

*If not using rapid rise or bread machine yeast, add sugar to warm water and sprinkle with yeast. Wait ten minutes for it to foam, then proceed with recipe. If it doesn't foam, throw it out and start over.

Challah Bread

3 eggs
1 cup milk
3 T butter
¼ cup sugar
1 ½ tsp salt
1 tsp yeast*
3 cups flour

Mix all ingredients together thoroughly in large bowl. Cover and refrigerate for at least 8 hours, up to 5 days.

Divide dough into three pieces, then roll out each piece (on floured surface) with your hands into a snake. Braid together (it's easier to braid bread if you start from the middle, braid one side, then braid the other). Place on oiled baking sheet. Cover, and let rise until doubled. Beat an egg with a T of water, then brush challah bread with it so it browns nicely. You can also sprinkle with poppy seeds at this point, if you like. Bake at 350F for 20-25 minutes.

*If not using rapid rise or bread machine yeast, add sugar to warm water and sprinkle with yeast. Wait ten minutes for it to foam, then proceed with recipe. If it doesn't foam, throw it out and start over.

Sour Cream Bread

The taste of this bread is incredible, so don't be put off by the unusual ingredients. The interior is soft with a wonderful texture, and the crust is crisp and browns to a beautiful color. Try it, you won't be sorry.

¾ cup water
1 cup sour cream
1 T olive or vegetable oil
1 ½ tsp salt
2 T sugar
1 ½ tsp yeast*
3 cups flour

Mix, in large bowl, two cups flour to the remaining ingredients. Beat with a wooden spoon for about 5 minutes, then add in remaining flour and mix thoroughly. Cover, and place in refrigerator for 8 hours hours, up to 5 days.

Stretch to roughly fit oiled loaf pan. Cover and let rise until doubled. Bake at 350F for 30-40 minutes. Let cool in pan for ten minutes, then move to rack and cool for at least 20 more.

*If not using rapid rise or bread machine yeast, add sugar to warm water and sprinkle with yeast. Wait ten minutes for it to foam, then proceed with recipe. If it doesn't foam, throw it out and start over.

Pumpernickel Bread

1 ½ cups water
2 T vegetable oil
¼ cup molasses
1 ½ tsp salt
2 tsp yeast*
2 T cocoa
1 cup all purpose or bread flour
1 cup rye flour
1 cup whole wheat flour

Stir all ingredients except flour together. Beat in flours one at the time, until thoroughly mixed. Cover, and refrigerate for at least 8 hours, for up to 5 days.

Stretch dough into rough rectangle and put into oiled loaf pan. Cover and let rise until doubled. Bake in 350F oven for 45 minutes.

*If not using rapid rise or bread machine yeast, add sugar to warm water and sprinkle with yeast. Wait ten minutes for it to foam, then proceed with recipe. If it doesn't foam, throw it out and start over.

One roll recipe. Anyway you make it, it's delicious.

Dinner Rolls

This versatile dinner roll recipe makes a lovely, soft roll with a chewy crust. It can be used to make Parker House Rolls, cloverleaf rolls, knots, snails, or crescents.

½ cup water
½ cup buttermilk
1/8 cup sugar
1 tsp salt
3 T softened butter
1 tsp yeast*
2 ½ cups flour

Mix all ingredients together and beat thoroughly with wooden spoon. Cover, and place in refrigerator for at least 8 hours, and up to 5 days.

Separate dough into 15 equal pieces.

- To make knot rolls: Use hands to roll each piece into a snake. Tie a knot in center, and tuck ends underneath.
- To make cloverleaf rolls: Separate each piece into three balls and drop into greased muffin cup.
- To make snails: Use hands to roll each piece into a snake. Coil into a snail shape.
- Parker House Rolls: Roll out into rectangle, and fold in half.
- To make crescent type rolls: Roll into a triangle, and roll up from the long end. Curve gently.

Cover rolls in oiled pan, and let rise in warm place until doubled. Brush rolls with melted butter before putting into 350F oven for about 25-30 minutes.

*If not using rapid rise or bread machine yeast, add sugar to warm water and sprinkle with yeast. Wait ten minutes for it to foam, then proceed with recipe. If it doesn't foam, throw it out and start over.

Russian Black Bread

This is a dark, dense bread. This is the way that Russians eat their bread – or so says my friend, who is Russian and gave me this recipe. It's delicious, and practically a meal in itself. You either like this kind of bread or you hate it, I have found. It's one of my favorites, and I just had to include it here. It's a little more difficult recipe, but totally worth it.

2 cups warm water
1/4 cup molasses
1/4 cup apple cider vinegar
4 T butter
2 T cocoa powder or 2 squares good baker's chocolate
1 T salt
1 T espresso powder or dark roast instant coffee

3 1/2 tsp yeast*
1/2 cup whole-wheat flour
3 cups rye flour
3 cups all-purpose or bread flour
2 tablespoons caraway seeds (optional. I actually grind the seeds and add them, because I don't like whole seeds in my bread)

Add water, molasses, vinegar, chocolate, salt, butter, and coffee (everything in top half of recipe) to pan on stove and stir over medium heat until everything melts together. Let sit until just warm, then add yeast and stir.

Combine flours and caraway seeds (if using) in large mixing bowl. Add yeast mixture and stir together until well blended. It's going to be a sticky dough, but not too wet. You want the dough to clear the sides of bowl while you're mixing, and if you're using a stand mixer, you want it to begin to work its way up the paddle.

Cover and refrigerate for at least 8 hrs or up to 5 days.

Pour dough onto floured surface, and shape into 2 loaves or form into 2 large rounds. Let rise in warm place until doubled, and cook at 350F for 45 to 50 minutes.

*If not using rapid rise or bread machine yeast, add sugar to warm water and sprinkle with yeast. Wait ten minutes for it to foam, then proceed with recipe. If it doesn't foam, throw it out and start over.

Whole Wheat Bread

1 ¼ cup water
2 T softened butter
¼ cup sugar or honey
1 ½ tsp salt
1 ½ cups all purpose flour
1 ½ cups whole wheat flour
1 ½ tsp yeast*

Mix half the flour with the rest of the ingredients, and beat with wooden spoon. Add in rest of flour. Cover, and refrigerate for at least 8 hours, up to 5 days.

Shape into a rough loaf and put into oiled loaf pan. Cover and let rise until doubled, then bake at 350F for 30-35 minutes.

*If not using rapid rise or bread machine yeast, add sugar to warm water and sprinkle with yeast. Wait ten minutes for it to foam, then proceed with recipe. If it doesn't foam, throw it out and start over.

Brioche

This isn't made in the traditional French way, but it's a great recipe for brioche. It's rich, soft, and buttery, and is a decadent treat. It's more of a batter than a dough, and may have to be scooped into the pan or muffin tins. Make sure the butter is really soft, so that it beats in well. You can melt it if you want, but make sure you let it cool before you add it. This recipe contains a lot of butter; you can actually reduce this amount by half if you like, without ruining the taste of the bread.

½ cup water
2 tsp yeast*
½ cup milk
1 cup softened butter
3 eggs
¼ cup sugar
1 tsp salt
4 cups flour

Into large bowl stir water, yeast, milk, butter, sugar, salt and 2 cups of the flour. Beat with wooden spoon for about 5 minutes. Add in eggs, one at a time, beating well after each addition. Add in the remaining flour, and beat until the batter is smooth. Cover, and refrigerate for at least 8 hours, for up to 5 days.

Spoon batter into buttered loaf pan or 24 muffin tins. Cover and let rise until doubled. Bake at 350F for 20-25 minutes for mini brioches, or 35 minutes for a loaf.

*If not using rapid rise or bread machine yeast, add sugar to warm water and sprinkle with yeast. Wait ten minutes for it to foam, then proceed with recipe. If it doesn't foam, throw it out and start over.

Seven Grain Cereal Bread

1 ½ cups water
¼ cup milk
2 tsp yeast*
3 T vegetable oil
3 T honey
1 ½ tsp salt
1 egg
1 cup whole wheat flour
2 ½ cups all purpose or bread flour
¾ cup 7 grain cereal

Mix half the flour with all other ingredients in a large bowl, beating thoroughly with a wooden spoon. Add in the rest of the flour. Cover, and refrigerate for at least 8 hours, for up to 5 days.

Shape into one large or two small loaves or boules. Place in well oiled pan or baking sheet. Cover, and let rise until doubled. For one large loaf, bake at 350F for 40 minutes. For two small loaves, reduce time to 30 minutes.

*If not using rapid rise or bread machine yeast, add sugar to warm water and sprinkle with yeast. Wait ten minutes for it to foam, then proceed with recipe. If it doesn't foam, throw it out and start over.

Naan Bread

Naan is an Indian flatbread, and it is delicious. It is made with yogurt, so the dough is smooth with a light tang. It's fried in the pan with a little oil or butter, and it blisters up as it cooks. It's thicker than a tortilla, and it's wonderful rolled around something like shredded chicken or used to scoop up curry.

½ cup water
2 tsp yeast*
1 tsp sugar
2 ½ cups flour
½ tsp salt
¼ cup vegetable oil
½ cup plain yogurt
1 egg

Beat together all the ingredients in one large bowl. Cover, and place in refrigerator for at least 4 hours, or up to 5 days.

Divide dough into 8 pieces and roll out thinly into a circle on floured surface. Heat an oiled or buttered skillet, and cook naan until it's blistered on the top and lightly browned on the bottom. Flip it over and cook the other side until lightly browned.

Cheesy Herb Bread

1 ½ cups water
¼ cup softened butter
1 ½ tsp salt
1 T sugar
2 tsp yeast*
2 ¾ cups all purpose or bread flour
1 cup whole wheat flour
1 minced garlic clove or 2 tsp garlic powder
2 tsp dried parsley (or about 2 T chopped fresh)
1 tsp dried basil (or 1 T chopped fresh)
½ cup grated Parmesan cheese
½ cup shredded Swiss, Cheddar or other cheese of your choice

Mix everything in large bowl except cheese and half the flour. Beat in cheeses, and remaining flour. Cover and place in refrigerator for at least 8 hours or overnight.

Divide dough and form into two boules or loaves and place in oiled pan or baking sheet. Bake at 350F for 45 minutes for one loaf, 30 minutes for two. Let cool completely before cutting.

*If not using rapid rise or bread machine yeast, add sugar to warm water and sprinkle with yeast. Wait ten minutes for it to foam, then proceed with recipe. If it doesn't foam, throw it out and start over.

Raisin Bran Bread

1 cup water
2 tsp yeast
¼ cup packed brown sugar
3 T softened butter
1 tsp salt
1 ½ cups raisin bran cereal
2 ¼ cups flour
½ cup raisins

Soak the raisins in the cup of water for about a half hour. Add in all other ingredients and mix thoroughly. This is a wet, sticky dough. Cover, and place in refrigerator for at least 8 hours or up to 5 days.

Put dough in oiled loaf pan. Cover and let rise until doubled in size. Bake at 350F for 30-35 minutes.

*If not using rapid rise or bread machine yeast, add sugar to warm water and sprinkle with yeast. Wait ten minutes for it to foam, then proceed with recipe. If it doesn't foam, throw it out and start over.

Oatmeal Bread

1 ¼ cups water
2 T vegetable oil
¼ cup sugar or honey
1 ½ tsp salt
½ cup oats (either quick or old-fashioned)
1 ½ tsp yeast*
2 ¾ cups flour

Mix all ingredients thoroughly in large bowl. Cover and place in refrigerator for at least 8 hours and up to 5 days.

Shape into loaf and put into oiled loaf pan. Cover and let rise until doubled. Bake at 350F for 35-40 minutes.

*If not using rapid rise or bread machine yeast, add sugar to warm water and sprinkle with yeast. Wait ten minutes for it to foam, then proceed with recipe. If it doesn't foam, throw it out and start over.

Extras, Extras, Extras

There are a lot of great quick breads or recipes that don't require yeast, or ones that don't need to be put in the refrigerator to rest and develop flavors before cooking. Quick breads and cakes use baking soda or baking powder or eggs to achieve a rise, and things like pasta don't use yeast or rise at all. I debated whether or not to include these recipes, but then decided that they had a place in this book. They're just too yummy to leave out.

I have several staple recipes that I can't do without, and I'm happy to share these recipes. They've brought a lot of enjoyment and deliciousness to my table over the years, and I hope that you and yours love them as much as I do. And feel free to do what all good cooks do: Experiment with these recipes, and let your imagination go wild. Make them truly yours.

Banana Bread

3 mashed bananas
2 beaten eggs
½ cup butter
¾ cup brown sugar
1 tsp vanilla
2 cups flour
1 tsp baking soda
½ tsp salt
½ cup chopped nuts *optional
1 tsp each of cinnamon, ginger, and nutmeg *optional

Preheat oven to 350F.

In large bowl, combine flour, baking soda, and salt. Cream butter and sugar in separate bowl, then stir in mashed banana, vanilla, and eggs. Stir butter mixture into flour along with nuts and spice (if using). Don't over-stir, and just stir it into it's mixed. Over-stirring can make quick breads tough and dense.

Bake in oiled loaf pan for 60 to 65 minutes, until a toothpick inserted into center of loaf comes out clean. Let bread cool in pan for 10 minutes, then turn out onto a wire rack to cool completely.

Pasta

Not everyone uses eggs in their pasta, but I think it gives it a richer, nicer taste. This can be used to make any type of pasta or dumplings, depending on how they are rolled out or cut. Changing from butter to olive oil in the recipe also changes the flavor just slightly. I usually use the olive oil when I'm making Italian style dishes, and the butter for dumplings. These can be dried and stored in an airtight container for up to a month. They're great fresh, though.

Just let dry for an hour or so before using in recipes, and remember that fresh pasta doesn't take even half the time to cook that regular pasta does. If you've just rolled it out and cut it into the shape that you want, more than a couple of minutes cooking time for thin pasta is overkill. If you wanted to make this pasta up right away and not wait for the refrigerator time, just knead it for ten minutes or so after letting it rest for a half hour, then roll out. The flavors are better when allowed to rest in the refrigerator for several hours, however. You can add anything you want to this recipe; I often add chopped basil or garlic.

2 ½ cups flour (spelt is best, but I often use all-purpose, and they still turn out great)
½ tsp salt
2 beaten eggs
½ cup milk
1 T butter or olive oil

Thoroughly mix all ingredients in large bowl. Cover, and place in refrigerator for at least 4 hours and up to 5 days.

On floured surface, roll out dough to desired thickness. Cut into desired shapes and let dry for two hours before cooking. For pasta, roll it out thin. You want it about a $1/16^{th}$ of an inch thick. A pizza cutter is the easiest way to cut it.

No-Fail Brownies

These really are no-fail brownies, and they're the best ones I've ever tasted. They are rich and chocolatey and decadent. It's a simple recipe, but follow it exactly (except for adjusting cooking times and heating, since everyone's oven is different). Variations are a different subject entirely, however. Cut in small pieces and roll in powdered sugar or cocoa. Swirl a sweet cream cheese filling on top, add in some caramel pieces (or swirl it in, too), add chocolate chips or peanut butter chips...the possibilities are endless. It's a great brownie recipe.

1 stick butter
1 cup sugar
¾ cup cocoa powder
¼ teaspoon salt
2 teaspoons vanilla
2 eggs (cold)
½ cup all-purpose flour
½ cup pecans or walnuts *optional

Preheat oven to 325F.

In glass heat-proof bowl, combine butter, sugar, salt, and cocoa. Put the bowl in a skillet full of water that has been brought to a gentle simmer. Stir occasionally until it's hot and melted together and shiny. Remove it from heat and let it cool until barely warm.

Beat in eggs one at a time until the batter is shiny and mixed. Add vanilla. Stir in flour until just mixed, then beat for about 30 strokes. Stir in nuts, if using.

Spread in well-oiled pan. Bake until knife inserted in center comes out just a little moist, for 20 to 25 minutes. Let the brownies cool completely before cutting, or they will fall apart.

Sweet Cornbread

1 cup flour
1 cup cornmeal
½ tsp baking soda
1 tsp baking powder
½ tsp salt
¼ cup sugar or honey
¼ cup applesauce
¾ cup milk
2 eggs

Preheat oven to 425F.

Mix dry ingredients in large bowl. In separate bowl, mix all wet ingredients. Combine, and pour into well-greased baking pan. Cook for 15 to 20 minutes, until lightly browned.

Best Chocolate Cake

This is the best chocolate cake I've ever eaten. It makes three layers. I usually use a chocolate ganache for icing (I'll add that on at the end of the recipe for you). It's rich and delicious and my go-to cake when I need one.

3 cups packed brown sugar
1 cup softened butter
4 eggs
2 2/3 cup all purpose flour
3/4 cup cocoa
1 T baking soda
1/2 tsp salt
1 1/3 cups sour cream
1 1/3 cups boiling water

Preheat oven to 350F.

In a mixing bowl, cream brown sugar and butter. Add eggs, one at a time, beating well after each addition. If using a mixer, beat on high speed or beat by hand until light and fluffy. Add vanilla. Combine flour, cocoa, baking soda and salt in separate bowl; add alternately with sour cream to creamed mixture. Mix just until combined, then stir in boiling water until blended. Pour into three greased and floured (or oiled, with parchment paper) 9' round baking pans.

Bake for about 35 minutes. Test by inserting toothpick in center; it's done when it comes out clean. Cool in pans for 10 minutes; remove to wire racks to cool completely.

Chocolate ganache icing

9 ounces good quality chocolate, chopped
1 cup heavy cream
1 T rum, Kahlua, or other liqueur *optional

Place chopped chocolate into a medium bowl. Heat the cream in a small sauce pan over medium heat. Bring just to a boil. Pour over the chopped chocolate, and whisk until smooth. Stir in liqueur if using.

You can use this as a glaze, as is, just by letting it cool slightly. Always start at the center of the cake and work outward. For a fluffy frosting, allow it to cool until thick, then whip with a whisk or mixer until light and fluffy.

CPSIA information can be obtained
at www.ICGtesting.com
Printed in the USA
269617LV00008B